Breaking Waves

Winslow Homer
Paints the Sea

ROBERT BURLEIGH   Paintings by WENDELL MINOR

NEAL PORTER BOOKS

HOLIDAY HOUSE / NEW YORK

Splash!
Sea spray flying up into mist!
Look!

WINTER.

Winslow looks at the sea.

Prouts Neck, Maine. Halfway down a rocky slope at the coast's edge, the artist gazes out, watching intently. He sees the dark, restless ocean stretching far into the blue-gray horizon.

A sudden wave breaks and splatters against the rocks below him, sending a chill shower against his face.

Still he watches. Something about this moment holds his attention. This wild struggle between two vast parts of nature locked in an endless battle.

Sea versus land. Land versus sea.

Winslow takes from inside his heavy coat a tiny notebook. He pauses, then with a small pencil, he scrawls—as he often does—a brief sentence: "You must wait," he prints roughly, "and wait patiently."

After a final look at the scene before him, Winslow turns and walks back up the slope, heading home. He will try to paint what he has seen.

Splash!
A dab of blue paint.
White drops scattering across the canvas.
Rough and rapid brush strokes. A wipe of the cloth.
Look!

Winslow looks at his painting on the easel in his studio.

He tilts it toward the light from the window, watching the colors change as the sunlight passes and the day darkens.

Blowing on his hands to warm them, he lifts the brush, thick with paint. With a firm hand he adds a bit of green.

Slowly, the painting shifts as layers of gray, white, and yellow magically transform into waves.

The painting is still—yet full of motion.

How can paint and canvas ever tell the true story of the vast and ever-changing ocean? Winslow doesn't know the answer, but he feels the puzzle patiently waiting deep within him. It has always been there.

He knows he must try.

"Oh what a friend chance can be— when it chooses."

Shimmer!
Light glittering on tiny whitecaps.
Sun and sea are dancing.
Look!

SPRING.

Winslow looks at the sea.

Like a sea captain steering his ship from the deck, Winslow paces back
and forth on the balcony of his studio house (he calls it his "piazza"),
gazing out toward the distant water.

How far out it is, that straight edge of sea!

He walks the path to the cliff's edge, watching the glimmer of water grow as he moves toward it. Perching on damp rocks or squatting on bits of sand and grass, he sees the waves lapping up just beneath the cliff, listens to their gentle and comforting rhythm.

Winslow never tires of wandering this coast. He knows every shrub, every clump of grass, every boulder. Each day the sea speaks to him, always with a slightly different voice.

He takes out a bit of charcoal and his notebook, sketching in a few quick lines on the page. The lines become waves breaking against rock. He slides the worn notebook into his satchel.

Winslow closes his eyes. A light mist caresses his cheeks and dampens his coat and shoes. He breathes in the faint, piney scent of the juniper trees.

When he opens his eyes again, the brilliant red of sunset tints the clouds above the edge of the horizon. Walking backward, as he sometimes does to avoid taking his eyes off a magnificent sight, he watches the sky turn pink and orange. Slowly, the sun dips down behind him to the west.

At last, the sky begins to gray. Winslow turns away and walks back up the path to his studio, colors throbbing in his mind's eye.

"The life that I have chosen gives me my full hours of enjoyment . . .
The Sun will not rise, or set, without my notice and thanks."

Shimmer!
Smear of pale yellow swerving against the black.
Dollop of orange mixed with midnight.
Look!

Winslow looks at his painting.

He scrapes the paper hard, adding a smooth wash of soft gray.

For a moment, he steps back from his easel. He ambles around the room, studying the few recent sketches tacked up on the walls.

Now! He returns to the easel. Rapidly, he mixes red and burnt orange hues on his palette, then the colors of wet rock and ocean: browns, blacks, blues, with a flash of white as his brush skims the surface. And on the page, the colors slowly turn—into ocean, rocks, glowing clouds.

How much time has passed? Minutes? Hours? Winslow doesn't know. When he is painting, he is aware of nothing but what he is trying to do.

"When you paint, try to put down exactly what you see. Whatever else you have to offer will come out anyway."

Calm.
Balmy breezes floating across the water.
Soft clouds dotting the sky.
Look!

SUMMER.

Winslow looks at the sea.

Fishing boats float like small toys in the faraway blue. The faint calls of children on the few beaches blend with the breeze. Visitors stroll the paths. In summer, many people visit this remote and lovely place.

He remembers the men and women he met when he lived for a time near the sea in Cullercoats, England: their struggle to salvage a life from the harsh sea, the way they hauled in the heavy nets, teeming with silvery fish, the hardship and pain of their difficult lives.

Yet there was a beauty in their elemental battle for survival that has stayed with him and moves him still. In fact, that stark beauty has led him to this place. It is why he never tires of this great subject of his: the force and power of the constantly changing ocean, now gleaming in the sun like a mirror.

How many moods this ocean has! All of them fascinate Winslow.
But a peaceful summer day doesn't always satisfy his soul as
much as a storm does!

Still, as he gazes out, this glorious summer afternoon delights him.

"All is lovely outside my house and inside my house and myself."

Calm.
Charcoal lines blending into a distant horizon.
Quick strokes of blue vibrating in the depths.
Look!

Winslow looks at his painting.

He has been working on this same picture for many weeks. Sometimes, he feels he will never get it right. He fears the ocean in his picture will never come to life. But this morning when he awoke, he knew what he has to do: scrape and begin again. Paint!

At noon, he stirs, puts down his brush. Stretching, he walks out onto his balcony. In the distance, he can see the faint outlines of the lighthouse on Wood Island. Butterflies flutter around the flowers that grow in his small garden. He returns to his easel.

Warm afternoon air wafts through the open window of his studio. He hears people walk by his house and pause by the door. But no visitors today— he is painting!

He is glad he put out his sign: "Mr. Homer is not at home." At last, all is quiet. He can work again.

"What they call talent is nothing but the capacity for doing
continuous hard work in the right way."

Roar!
Stormy skies swirling above the sea.
A gust of wind twisting the trees.
Look!

FALL.

Winslow looks at the sea, pounding like a distant drum.

The boom and crash of water against the shore sings Winslow to sleep at night and shakes him awake in the morning. The panes of glass in the windows shudder as if about to break. Nor'easters are brewing far out in the ocean. Walls of wind take his breath away.

His white-haired terrier, Sam, scampers by his side as they fight the gale all the way down the worn path.

Elated, Winslow steps to the very rim of the rocks, once more feeling the force of wind and waves stir his soul: majestic, free, wild, untamed—forever!

It's what he feels when he paints. It's what he wants someone to feel when they view his paintings. The power of nature—and the power of art.

"Look at nature, work independently, and solve your own problems."

Roar!
A curl of wave curving like a question mark on
the page.
Smears of paint transforming the picture.
Look!

Winslow looks at his painting.

Holding his hands before the fireplace,

he rubs them together. A pot of stew simmers on the fire.

As he sits in his chair by the window, sees visitors, or talks with his father or

brother, he is always wondering at the back of his mind: How? How will I

do it? And he feels the call: back to his easel, back to his paints.

Each time he finishes a painting, for a moment he thinks he has done it.

But then Winslow feels an urge to try again: to stretch a new canvas, to

unwrap a sketchpad, to open fresh tubes of paint.

"At any moment, I am liable to paint a good picture."

Winter again.

Winslow looks at the sea.

Or is he looking at his painting?

Winslow looks at his painting.

Or is he looking at the sea?

At last, the two are becoming one!

Winslow sets out a fresh canvas on his easel.

Look!

More About Winslow Homer

Who was Winslow Homer?

Born in Boston, Massachusetts, on February 24, 1836, Winslow became an artist the hard way! His father was a businessman, so Winslow didn't come from a family of professional artists—though his mother was an accomplished amateur painter and encouraged her son's artistic pursuits. From the time he was a boy, Homer had a talent for drawing and art. But he didn't become a great artist all at once.

Photograph of Winslow Homer (ca. 1900), Bowdoin College Museum of Art
(Gift of the Homer Family)
This photograph shows Winslow with his easel in front of his painting Gulf Stream, *which was begun in Florida but finished at Prouts Neck. The painting shows an African-American sailor resting after struggling to keep his boat afloat in a raging, shark-filled sea (you can see the shark detail in the lower right corner of the painting).*

How did he become an artist?

At the age of nineteen, Winslow learned the trade of printmaking by becoming an apprentice to a lithographer. But young Winslow was largely self-taught as an artist. He worked diligently as an illustrator, beginning his career in the 1850s by drawing scenes from life around him. Then, during the Civil War in the early 1860s, *Harper's Weekly* magazine sent Winslow into the heat of war to sketch officers and soldiers—even the wounded—both on and off the battlefield. Those sketches helped people understand life at the front lines.

What is success?

In the years immediately after the war, Winslow became well known as a portrayer of everyday American life. He drew and painted children playing, people driving their carriages, families picnicking,

Nassau (ca. 1899), the Metropolitan Museum of Art, New York City
When Winslow went south in the winter, he didn't stop painting! He made trips to various locations, including Nassau in the Bahamas. There he was again attracted to the sea—and those whose lives depended upon it. Here we see local Black fishermen, descendants of slaves, setting out in their sailboats from a beach strewn with wreckage. Winslow's skill as a watercolorist is clear as he suggests waves, boats, and sailors with just a few deft strokes of the brush.

couples dancing, and boys playing sports. He also painted portraits of people (including a number of African Americans, who were often ignored by other artists of that time). Winslow's work was published in books and magazines. And he was paid! At a fairly early age, he was considered a successful artist.

What next?

But Winslow wanted something more. In 1881, at age forty-five, he decided to travel to England. He stayed for two years—not in fashionable London, but in Cullercoats, a coastal fishing village far removed from other artists—and from the art world itself. On the wild coast near the North Sea, he became more deeply connected to the beauty and power of the ocean, which had always drawn him. At the same time, he saw firsthand the strength and bravery of the local people—the men and women whose livelihoods depended on the ever-changing sea—and his painting began to change accordingly. Gradually, Winslow became aware of a more profound world than the one he had known before. It was almost as if the sea had spoken—directly to him!

Basket of Clams (ca. 1873), the Metropolitan Museum of Art, New York City
Two young boys carry a basket of clams near beached boats in Gloucester, Massachusetts,
in this bright watercolor. Though Homer was not married and had no children himself, his
art often portrays children playing or performing simple everyday tasks.

Where to go?

Returning to the United States, he at first tried to continue his career in New York City, a center for many successful artists at that time. But now, to Winslow, this world seemed empty and shallow. Where to go? What to do? Some members of his family, including his brother and father, had bought property on a high, barren peninsula off the coast of Maine called Prouts Neck (so-called because, when seen from above, it is shaped somewhat like the neck and head of a person— see map on page 39.) Soon Winslow decided to move there, too.

A new life, a new art.

Now Winslow began a quite different life, leaving the sophisticated society world of New York. His new home was a small former stable and carriage house (complete with rough living quarters and an art studio) around 100 feet from the edge of a cliff that overlooked the

Atlantic Ocean. Living here, he would listen to the crash of water against the rocky walls, feel the howling of the wind, take long walks at every time of the year, and paint the wide horizons and giant waves that changed constantly—often, hour by hour. Winslow made a rule that he would stay in Prouts Neck until his "water bucket froze solid!" But in the heart of winter, he sometimes left his new home, heading to Florida and the Caribbean islands. Always an avid fisherman, he enjoyed fishing in the Bahamas—and also occasionally traveled to the streams and forests of the Adirondacks in upstate New York. In all these places, he created lasting paintings.

A great artist at last.

But the sea at Prouts Neck—Winslow's most compelling subject— always called him back. Finally recognized by critics and the public as the powerful American artist that he was, Winslow continued to live and work primarily at Prouts Neck. His final oil painting (called *Driftwood*) shows a man—perhaps the artist himself?—near the water's edge, gazing at the ocean as it pounds against the rocks. Winslow had completed his work.

Weatherbeaten (ca. 1894), the Portland Museum of Art, Portland, Maine
Weatherbeaten, indeed! Winslow rarely missed a chance to portray the endless struggle
between the sea and the land. Here a wave is crashing at the foot of the high rock formation
where Prouts Neck meets the Atlantic. Far off, the faint, light gray spot seems to suggest
that the sun is about to rise. Homer didn't set up an easel just once and paint the sea as it
smashes against the shore. He made many visits to the top and even the foot of the high
cliffs, thinking and sketching—always looking for slightly different angles. Everything came
together when he began to paint the scene in his studio. For Winslow, every detail counted!

Winslow Homer died on September 29, 1910.

But Winslow's work lives on. Today you can find his paintings on the walls and websites of most major art museums in the United States, including the Metropolitan Museum of Art in New York City, the Museum of Fine Arts, Boston, and the National Gallery of Art in Washington, D.C. You can also visit Winslow's studio at Prouts Neck, which has been recently restored and is open to the public. The Portland Museum, located in Portland, Maine, runs tours of Homer's studio and also has a fine collection of his paintings. And do you like traveling? Well, the next time you're in Paris, you can even stop in at the Musée d'Orsay and see Winslow's beautiful painting *Summer Night*!

Gloucester Harbor *(ca. 1873), Nelson-Atkins Museum of Art, Kansas City, Missouri*
In this early and serene oil painting of children in a rowboat with a backdrop of sailboats, a rosy bank of clouds is reflected in the calm water. This is another example of Homer's close attention to the life, light, and color around him.

Life at Prouts Neck

Stable or studio? Winslow's studio was a renovated stable/carriage house. It had been near "The Ark," the name of his brother's house. Winslow even had the carriage house moved 100 feet away from The Ark, so that he could be nearer the ocean that overlooked the cliff walk and the coast.

Northeaster *(ca. 1895), the Metropolitan Museum of Art, New York City*
In some of Winslow's sea paintings, the ocean seems to take on a life of its own. The blue-white wave rising up on the left side of this picture appears ready to smash against the rocks. You can almost hear the thunderous roar.

A simple life. Two rooms on the ground floor of his studio house contained a fireplace, a simple table, and a few chairs. A larger space on the second floor led out to a long balcony with a roof from which he could gaze at the sea, which he called the piazza. There was no electricity or central heating in the small building. Winters could be tough! Winslow once confessed: "I made a mistake in not getting a larger stove!"

The hermit of Prouts Neck. Winslow sometimes promoted his image as "the hermit of Prouts Neck" by erecting signs outside of his studio or near where he was working to keep people away. The signs said things like "SNAKES! SNAKES! MICE!" or "Mr. Homer Is Not at Home." But that was only one part of his personality!

A generous and kind fellow. Winslow also was known for being generous and kind to the local villagers—a community of family, friends, and local fishermen. In this unusual setting, he found companions and a sense of belonging.

West Point Prouts Neck *(ca. 1900), The Clark Museum, Williamstown, Massachusetts*
The beautiful red-orange sunset is starting to fade, but the endless struggle of the sea against the shore continues. Homer's watchful eye was always on the alert for a moment of pure poetry.

Lunch anyone? But his life wasn't all rough-and-tumble! During the summers, Winslow would raise a flag on his balcony at lunchtime, so that the nearby Checkley Hotel staff would see it and know it was time to deliver lunch to his studio door!

An artist and a chef. Winslow was a good cook, too, and cooked stews and soups over the fire in the fireplace of his studio. He also grew vegetables in a garden near the studio.

A dapper dresser. Although Winslow typically worked in simple, everyday clothes, when he entertained visitors or had outings with his family, he wore fancy suits that he ordered from Boston clothing stores. Sometimes, people who didn't know him thought at first glance he was a stockbroker!

An artist, not just a copier. Local villagers who looked at Winslow's paintings would sometimes tell him how to correct "mistakes" in his pictures! That's because he didn't always paint exactly what was

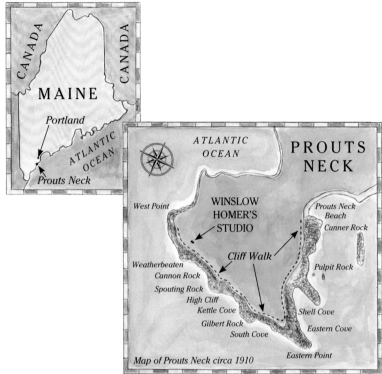

Map of Prouts Neck circa 1910

there. Sometimes, he made slight changes in the scene and in his early sketches to make the final work dramatic and fit his vision.

About Prouts Neck

Prouts Neck first appeared to Europeans on a map by Samuel de Champlain, who had explored New England in 1604. For many years, Prouts Neck was known as Black Point because its forests were so dark.

When Homer's brother Arthur first visited Prouts Neck in the 1870s, it was just a small fishing village in Maine surrounded by wild cliffs. With its special combination of natural beauty, seascapes, and rock formations, the small peninsula slowly became a popular East Coast summer destination—and in fact it still is.

Prouts Neck residents are called "Neckers." People who live there simply call it "Prouts." There were seven inns at Prouts Neck when Winslow was living there, but there's only one today. Many wealthy families have summered at Prouts Neck over the years, including the Rockefellers and the Carnegies.

Bibliography

There are, of course, numerous books about Winslow Homer, and almost all of them contain pictures of his art. These are just a few such books:

Beam, Philip C., *Winslow Homer at Prout's Neck*. Lanham, Maryland: Down East Books, 2014. (Originally published by Little, Brown, 1966)

Johns, Elizabeth, *Winslow Homer: The Nature of Observation*. University of California Press, 2002.

Venezia, Mike, *Winslow Homer*. New York: Children's Press, A Division of Scholastic, Inc., 2004. (A short book on Winslow Homer aimed at children.)

Denenberg, Thomas A., ed., *Weatherbeaten: Winslow Homer and Maine*. Yale University and Portland Museum of Art, Maine, 2012.

Where to see Homer's work

Portland Museum of Art
https://www.portlandmuseum.org/homer

The Metropolitan Museum of Art
https://www.metmuseum.org/TOAH/hd/homr/hd_homr.htm

The Art Institute of Chicago
https://archive.artic.edu/homer/artwork/16818

Smithsonian American Art Museum
https://americanart.si.edu/artist/winslow-homer-2283

Museum of Fine Arts Boston
https://collections.mfa.org/objects/31042

Los Angeles County Museum of Art
https://collections.lacma.org/node/164648

To Jen, who loves art —R.B.

For Florence —W.M.

Neal Porter Books

Text copyright © 2021 by Robert Burleigh
Illustrations copyright © 2021 by Wendell Minor
All Rights Reserved
HOLIDAY HOUSE is registered in the U.S. Patent and Trademark Office.
Printed and bound in February 2021 by C & C Offset, Shenzhen, China.
The artwork for this book was created with watercolor and gouache on 4 ply Strathmore Bristol paper.
Book design by Jennifer Browne
www.holidayhouse.com
First Edition
10 9 8 7 6 5 4 3 2 1

Library of Congress Cataloging-in-Publication Data

Names: Burleigh, Robert, author. | Minor, Wendell, illustrator.
Title: Breaking Waves : Winslow Homer paints the sea / by Robert Burleigh ; illustrated by Wendell Minor.
Description: First edition. | New York : Holiday House, 2021. | "A Neal Porter book." | Audience: Ages 4 to 8 | Audience: Grades K–1 | Summary: "A picture book about painter Winslow Homer's fascination with waves and the ocean"— Provided by publisher.
Identifiers: LCCN 2020025785 | ISBN 9780823447022 (hardcover)
Subjects: LCSH: Homer, Winslow, 1836-1910—Themes, motives—Juvenile literature. | Waves in art—Juvenile literature. | Sea in art—Juvenile literature.
Classification: LCC ND237.H7 B87 2021 | DDC 704.9/437—dc23
LC record available at https://lccn.loc.gov/2020025785

ISBN 978-0-8234-4702-2 (hardcover)